BIRMINGHAM
IN THE
SEVENTIES

Alton & Jo Douglas

Typical of the adventurous spirit of the seventies, the 2007 Space Age fashion store creates an imaginary lunar landscape, High Street, 30th November 1971.

© 2001 Alton and Jo Douglas
ISBN 1 85858 205 9
Published by Brewin Books Ltd., Doric House, 56 Alcester Road, Studley, Warwickshire B80 7LG.
Printed by Warwick Printing Co. Ltd., Theatre Street, Warwick CV34 4DR.
Layout by Alton and Jo Douglas
All Rights Reserved

A mixture of the old and new. Coventry Road, between Cyril Road and Henshaw Road, Small Heath, 16th March 1973.

Front Cover: Morecambe and Wise receive an affectionate welcome as they arrive to open the Downsway supermarket, Grosvenor Shopping Centre, Northfield, 27th November 1970.

Contents

BREWIN BOOKS LTD

Doric House, 56 Alcester Road,
Studley, Warwickshire B80 7LG

Tel: 01527 854228 Fax: 01527 852746

Vat Registration No. 705 0077 73

Dear Nostalgic,

Was it only yesterday? Well, first of all you have to convince yourself that the seventies actually started over thirty years ago. Then you have to work out exactly what you were doing at that time. Personally, I have a big hole in my Birmingham-seventies-consciousness as Jo and I started the decade by getting married in Weston-Super-Mare and then, as a professional comedian, I appeared in long summer seasons in Blackpool, Weston, Bexhill-on-Sea and Shanklin, pantomimes, cabaret, television, radio and lengthy theatre tours all over this sceptred isle. As far as our city was concerned a lot of the rebuilding had been done but there was plenty still to do. Life was fast and constantly changing so let's rewind to the seventies to see if you can find the YOU that used to be.

Yours, in friendship,

Alton

The Green, Kings Norton, 1970.

Handsworth Technical College, Friary Road, 2nd January 1970.

THE TOP 20 POPS

Last week	this week		
1	1	TWO LITTLE BOYS	Rolf Harris (Columbia)
7	2	TRACY	The Cuff Links (M.C.A.)
3	3	MELTING POT	The Blue Mink (Philips)
4	4	ALL I HAVE TO DO IS DREAM	Bobbie Gentry and Glen Campbell (Capitol)
2	5	RUBY, DON'T TAKE YOUR LOVE TO TOWN	Kenny Rogers and The First Edition (Reprise)
6	6	SUSPICIOUS MINDS	Elvis Presley (R.C.A.)
5	7	SUGAR, SUGAR	The Archies (R.C.A.)
9	8	GOOD OLD ROCK 'N' ROLL	The Dave Clark Five (Columbia)
17	9	REFLECTIONS OF MY LIFE	The Marmalade (Decca)
8	10	YESTER-ME, YESTER-YOU, YESTERDAY	Stevie Wonder (Tamla Motown)
10	11	WITHOUT LOVE	Tom Jones (Decca)
14	12	THE LIQUIDATOR	The Harry J. All-Stars (Trojan)
11	13	WINTER WORLD OF LOVE	Engelbert Humperdinck (Decca)
12	14	THE ONION SONG	Marvin Gaye and Tammi Terrell (Tamla Motown)
16	15	LEAVIN' (DURHAM TOWN)	Roger Whittaker (Columbia)
18	16	SOMEDAY WE'LL BE TOGETHER AGAIN	Diana Ross and The Supremes (Tamla Motown)
—	17	COME AND GET IT	The Bad Finger (Apple)
—	18	FRIENDS	The Arrival (Decca)
15	19	GREEN RIVER	The Creedence Clearwater Revival (Liberty)
18	20	LONELINESS	Des O'Connor (Columbia)

Burlington Street, Aston, 1970.

Singer, Donald Peers, starring in "Aladdin", serves tea in his dressing room to Myra Davenport (winner of a Heart-throb Competition) and her husband David, Alexandra Theatre, 31st January 1970.

Chillinghome Road, Bromford, 14th February 1970.

Hurst Street, 18th February 1970.

New Street, 16th March 1970.

As Cadbury's factory tour service comes to an end, after 67 years, the current group of guides get together for the last time, 28th April 1970.

Champagne for "Miss City Centre", Christine Jones, poured out by the Lord Mayor, Coun. Neville Bosworth, at the Spring Festival, 18th May 1970.

The newly launched lifeboat, "City of Birmingham", Exmouth, May 1970.

The UNITED BIRMINGHAM HOSPITALS
The GENERAL HOSPITAL
ACCIDENT & EMERGENCY DEPT.

APPOINTMENT CARD

SERIAL NUMBER   2/   81547

21 MAY 1970

NAME.................EVANS.

Before leaving the Hospital please arrange your next appointment at the Registration Counter.

PRESERVE THIS CARD AND SHOW IT ON EACH ATTENDANCE

For date and time of next attendance see reverse of Card

Throwing coins in the fountain, The Minories, May 1970.

As part of the annual fete at Mayfield Special School, the Headmaster, Michael Duncan, serenades the pupils, Heathfield Road, Perry Barr, May 1970.

Strikers at the Dunlop factory vote, almost unanimously, to continue the stoppage over equal pay with other Midland car workers, 28th May 1970.

BIRMINGHAM COUNTY FOOTBALL ASSOCIATION
REFEREES' COMMITTEE

This is to certify that

Mr. A.J.Jennings. of 309, Gristhorpe Road, Birmingham, 29.

having made progress in his refereeing ability, has satisfied the Birmingham County Football Association Referees' Committee as to his competence to be designated as a Class One Referee, and his name has been entered as such in the Registers of the Association.

Date 29th. May, 1970.

Chairman (Referees' Committee)

Secretary of the Association

Rea Street Day Nursery, Deritend, c 1970.

Playtime at the base of a Ladywood tower block, 29th May 1970.

9

Old Square, June 1970.

Heralding the start of the Festival in Calthorpe Park,
Balsall Heath, c 1970.

Coventry Road, Small Heath, 1st June 1970.

A REVOLT by Birmingham housewives against proposed rent and rate rises began in the city's Newtown shopping centre yesterday.

Mrs. Mary Rome, of Elizabeth Fry House, Ladywood, has written an open letter to the Housing Minister, Mr. Anthony Greenwood, and has begun a 10,000-signature petition signed only by housewives, complaining about rent and rate increases.

BIRMINGHAM PARISH CHURCH
(St Martin's - in - the - Bull Ring)

The Churchwardens Invite you to

A FAREWELL GATHERING

for

Canon & Mrs. Bryan Green

on

MONDAY, 22nd JUNE, 1970, at 8 p.m.

R.S.V.P.

Guests are requested to be seated by 7.45 p.m.
and bring this invitation with you

Alcester Road, Moseley, 1970.

Co-operative Insurance Society agents march along New Street to publicise their dispute over expenses, 15th July 1970.

11

Dangerous times in the partly demolished section of Somerset Street, Vauxhall, 11th August 1970.

Lancaster Circus, with the Central Fire Station right of centre, 12th August 1970.

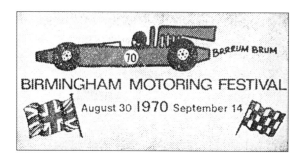

Maryland Avenue, Ward End, 1970.

Holidaymakers finally board a coach, after a hold-up due to an industrial dispute involving drivers, Digbeth Bus Station, 12th September 1970.

Soldiers of the 35th (South Midland) Signal Regiment take part in the Freedom of the City ceremony, 12th September 1970.

Edwardian bonnets on show at the Olde Tyme Music Hall, Harborne and Quinton Community Centre, Ridgacre Road, 16th September 1970.

14

ACOCKS GREEN ● Warwick. — 705 0766. — Bekhim Fehim, Charles Arnavour, THE ADVENTURERS (X) 3.30, 7.35. Full Supporting Programme 2.40, 6.25.

DUDLEY ROAD ● Grove. — Paul Newman, Joanne Woodward, Winning (U) 2.40, 5.30, 8.15. Selection of short features. L.P. 7.35.

ERDINGTON ● ABC Palace. — James Garner, Eva Marie Saint, Grand Prix (A) 7.20 (Sat. 3.55).

GREAT BARR ● Beacon. — Where Eagles Dare (A), 7.43. Mon., Tues., Sat. 2.58. The Question (A). 7.15. M.T.W.S. 2.30. Childs Club Sat. 10-12. Ad. 1/-.

HANDSWORTH. Elite. — Carry On Cleo (A), 5.30, 8.40; Carry On Jack (A). 7.10. Thurs: Hercules Against the Moon Men (U). Fri.: Midnight Movie 11.0: Cage Of Doom (X). Closed Sat. for private show.

KING'S HEATH ● Kingsway — Paul Newman, Joanne Woodward Winning (A). 5.25, 8.14. Mats. Mon, Wed. Sat. 2.40. L.P. 7.31.

KING'S NORTON ● 458 1079. Paul Newman, Joanne Woodward Winning (A) 5.20, 8.10 (Mon., Sat. 2.30) L.C.P. 7.20.

OLTON CINEMA ● 706 0593. — Paul Newman, Joanne Woodward Winning (A) 5.30, 8.15 (Wed., Sat. 2.45). Prospect of Iceland (U) 7.30 (Wed. Sat. 4.45).

PERRY BARR ● Clifton.—Paul Newman, Joanne Woodward, Winning (A), 5.41, 8.22, M.W.S. 3.0; The Pipeliners (U), 7.42. M.W.S. 2.20. 5.0. Childs Club Sat. 10-12. Adm. 1/-

QUINTON ● Essoldo — 422 2562 —Retained for a 2nd week. Richard Burton, Clint Eastwood, Where Eagles Dare (A). sep. perfs. (excl. Tues.) 2.30, 7.30. Tues. 2.30, 7.45. Circle 9/- (Bkble Evgs) Stalls 7/1 (unreserved) Child half price all perfs. (O.A.P. 2/6. mats. Mon to Fri). Box Office 2-8.30. Regret no phone bkgs.

SALTLEY. Rock 327 0476. — Carrol Baker, Apranoia (X), 5.50, 8.50. Mon. 2.50; 99 Women (X), 7.20 (M. 4.20). Th. Destination Gobi (U).

SELLY OAK ● ABC. — James Garner, GRAND PRIX (A), 3.55, 7.20. L.P. 7.0.

SHELDON ●—Richard Burton, WHERE EAGLES DARE (A). Sep perfs. eve. D.O. 6.50. Comm. 7.20. Mats. M.W.S. 2.30.

SHIRLEY ● Odeon, 744 1183. — Paul Newman, Winning (A), 2.35. 5.25, 8.20: The Pipeliners (U), 4.40, 7.30. No mat Tues. D.O. 5.10. Fri. Late Show D.O. 10.45 Trauma (X)

SOLIHULL ● Cinema 705 0398.— Where Eagles Dare (A), 7.35. D.O. 6.45. mats. Wed, Sat. 2.48. Sep perfs. Balcony 9/-, child 4/6. Stalls 7/-, child 3/6 (O.A.P. 2/6 mats only).

SPARKBROOK ● ABC.—James Garner. Eve Marie Saint. GRAND PRIX (A), 12.50, 4.15, 7.35. L.C.P. 7.15.

SPARKBROOK. Waldorf.—Kirk Douglas. A Lovely Way To Go (A); James Drury, The Young Warriors (A). Thurs: Jean Marias, Diamond Rush (A)

STOCKLAND GREEN ● Plaza— Night After Night After Night (X). 5.45. 9.0. Mats. Mon. Sat. 2.0: Cave Of The Living Dead (X), 7.20.

SUTTON COLDFIELD ● ABC.— Richard Burton, Where Eagles Dare (A), 7.30. mats. Mon. Sat. 2.0. Front circle bookable for evenings.

SUTTON COLDFIELD ● Odeon. —Paul Newman, Winning (A), 2.45. 5.35, 8.25. The Pipeliners (U), 2.0, 4.50, 7.40. Friday late horror show at 11.0 p.m.

WARD END ● Beaufort.— Richard Burton, Clint Eastwood, Where Eagles Dare (A), sep. perfs. 7.10, mats. Mon., Wed., Sat., 2.30.

WARD END. Capitol.—Paul Newman, Joanne Woodward. Winning (A), 5.20, 8.15. Mon., Sat., 2.30. Full supporting programme at 7.20.

WARLEY ● Astra. 552 1120.— The Sound of Music (U), one perf. starting 6.30. mats. Wed., Sat. 2.0. Advance booking Friday late show, 10.0: The Herion Gang (X).

WEST BROMWICH CINEMAS-

KINGS ● 553 0614.—Doctor in Trouble (A), Colour, 2.0, 5.25. 8.50. OSS 117 Murder for Sale (A), Colour, 3.40. 7.0.

IMPERIAL ● 553 0192.—Mick Jagger, Ned Kelly (AA), Colour, 2.0, 5.15. 8.35. Christopher George, Massacre Harbour (U), Colour, 3.45, 7.0.

REDDITCH CINEMA

DANILO ● 739 2572.—Doctor in Trouble (A), 5.30, 8.50. M., T., S., 2.10; OSS 117 Murder for Sale (A), 7.5. M., Th., S.,3.45.

HALESOWEN CINEMA

LYTTLETON ● 550 1448.—David Bradley, Kes (U), 8.20. Sat. 4.50; The 1000 Plane Raid (U), 6.40.

CRADLEY HEATH CINEMAS

ROYAL ●—Kes (U), 8.13, Mon., Tues., Fri., Sat., 4.30. The 1,000 Plane Raid (U), 6.25.

STRATFORD-UPON-AVON

PICTURE HOUSE ● 2622.— Warren Mitchell. All the Way Up (AA), 2.50, 5.40, 8.25. Last complete performance 7.20.

KIDDERMINSTER CINEMA

A.B.C. ● 562 2612. — The Wild Bunch (X). M/S. 1.50. 4.40. 7.40. Tu., Th., Fri. 7.50. Wed. 8.20 only; Support prog. 7.30. Mon, Sat. 4.30.

Warwick Road, Acocks Green, 1970.

Mr Hanson, General Manager of Lewis's, discusses the
company's award scheme for students with some of the winners,
29th October 1970.

Rear of Clevedon Road, Balsall Heath,
5th November 1970.

Grestone Avenue, Handsworth Wood, 7th December 1970.

Cranes Park Road, Sheldon, 8th December 1970.

1971

Rear of Sampson Road North, Camp Hill, 27th January 1971.

Rear of Sandy Lane, Sparkbrook, 27th January 1971.

Camp Hill, 27th January 1971.

Decimalisation arrives in Birmingham,
four days early, 11th February 1971.

Small Heath Police Station, Coventry Road,
14th February 1971.

Paradise Circus, with the new Central Library under construction in the centre, 1971.

The Broadway, with Davey Road on the right, Perry Barr, February 1971.

BIRMINGHAM'S latest section of motorway was officially opened today.

It cuts minutes off the drive to work for hundreds of city commuters.

The £4,000,000 stretch of the M6 link from Castle Bromwich to Coleshill will relieve one of the worst rush hour bottle-necks.

Smooth access

The five-mile motorway section by-passes the heavily congested Newport Road between Little Packington and Castle Bromwich to provide a smooth traffic access from the east.

But despite advantages to local traffic there was no fanfare or ceremony to open the new road today—because it is still an isolated section of the Midland links motorway scheme.

Members of The University of Birmingham Review Body, with the Rt. Hon. Jo Grimond, MP (centre) 1971.

The reshaping of Victoria Square takes place on the site of Galloways Corner, 22nd February 1971.

The landscaping nears completion, Victoria Square/New Street, 26th March 1971.

The Black Horse, Bristol Road South, Northfield, 1971.

Smithfield Wholesale Fruit and Vegetable Market, March 1971.

Gosta Green, 1971. The white building, occupied here by the Auto Spring Company, had previously been used as the BBC Television Studios.

ON a Royal visit that proved to be a massive " meet the people " tour, the Queen said this afternoon: " My, how Birmingham has changed since the last time I was here."

The Queen and the Duke of Edinburgh were in the city to open the £35,000,000 Inner Ring Road. Earlier she visited Chelmsley Wood where, it was estimated that more than 30,000 of the town's 45,000 population lined the route.

The Queen chats to onlookers, Colmore Row, 7th April 1971.

A NEW-TYPE battle of the sexes flared at the City of Birmingham College of Education, Edgbaston, today, after a group of boys formed a " smarten-up brigade " and told the girls: " You're too scruffy."

They say the girls, who outnumber them three to one, are drab dressers. Too many women slouch about in faded jeans and sloppy sweaters, they claim.

The Queen at the opening of the Inner Ring Road, 7th April 1971.

Shopping Precinct, Shawsdale Road, Castle Bromwich, 27th May 1971.

Time to pose for an anniversary picture, Cromwell Hall, Evangelistic Mission Church, Heath Green Road, Winson Green, June 1971.

Pershore Road/Hazelwell Road, Stirchley, 1971.

Soho Road, Handsworth, 1971.

Moseley Sunday First Cricket Eleven, July 1971.

On their way to a West End opening the girls of "The Avengers"
cast stop off at the Birmingham Theatre, 18th July 1971.
Incidentally, by 1972 the theatre had once again reverted to being
known as the Hippodrome.

Shoppers at the first day of the new C&A store, Corporation Street, 19th July 1971.

Raddlebarn Road, Selly Oak, 24th July 1971.

Charnbury Crescent, Yardley, 1971.

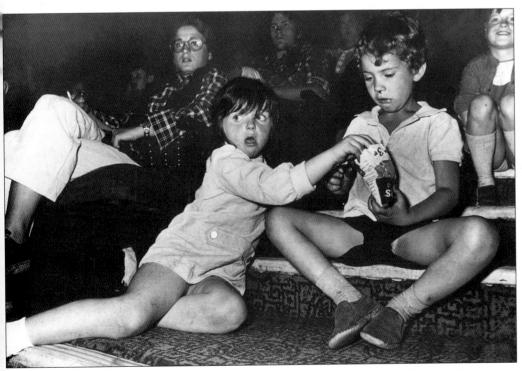

A special showing of children's films courtesy of the Holidays at Home charity,
Cinephone, Bristol Street, 31st July 1971.

Finnemore Road, Bordesley Green, September 1971.

Queslett Road/Walsall Road, Great Barr,
17th September 1971.

Common Lane/Church Road, Sheldon, 1971.

Temple Row, 1971.

Princess Margaret meets the cast of "First Impressions" at the official opening of the new Repertory Theatre, 20th October 1971.

Dennis Price, currently appearing on television as Jeeves, the butler (in the P.G. Wodehouse series), serves the first pint at "The Trusty Servant", Chelmsley Wood's newest pub, 28th October 1971.

LISTENERS will hear "Goodnight, everybody" spoken for the last time on Saturday from the B.B.C.'s Studio Centre in Broad Street, Birmingham.

Radio's leave-taking will follow television's farewell 24 hours earlier.

Broad Street, home of Midland broadcasting since 1926, is switching off.

From Monday all programmes in sound and vision will go on the air from the £6,000,000 Broadcasting Centre at Pebble Mill.

With the exception of some recorded material, all the television will be in colour.

Studio Centre has logged more than 17,000 radio news bulletins against some 2,000 by its junior, television.

THE COST OF LIVING IN 1971	
1lb of potatoes	3½p
1lb of butter	25p
20 Players cigarettes	31p
Instant coffee (4oz jar)	28½p
1lb of streaky bacon	29p
Gallon of petrol	33½p

Edgbaston Shopping Centre, Five Ways, 1st December 1971.

High Street, opposite Union Street, December 1971.

Les Dawson, and the dancers appearing in "Mother Goose", Alexandra Theatre, 20th December 1971.

1972

The University of Birmingham, 1972.

Reconstruction taking place in Priory Ringway, with Lewis's on the extreme right, 14th January 1972.

The workforce takes a breather as Spaghetti Junction nears completion, 1972.

Gas Street Basin, 1972.

Perry Barr Shopping Precinct, 1972.

Station Road, Stechford, 12th February 1972.

Corporation Street, 14th February 1972.

Thelma Yeomans, retiring after ten years as Division Commissioner of Guides and Brownies in Ladywood, receives a bouquet from Julie Baker, Trefoil House, Lee Bank, 23rd February 1972.

Bull Street, March 1972.

Rear of Brearley Street, Handsworth.

Comedian, Ken Goodwin, gets the Birmingham Motor Show off to a flying start, Bingley Hall, 1st April 1972.

Gert and Daisy.

Brays Road/Sheldon Heath Road, Sheldon, 1972.

Witton Road/Nelson Road, Aston, 12th April 1972.

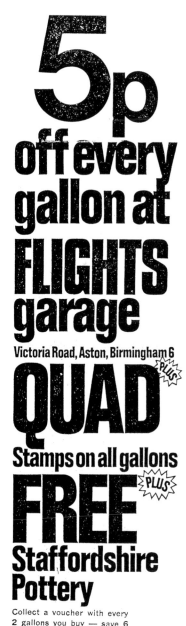

St George's (Church of England) Junior School football team, winners of the President's Trophy, Great Hampton Row, 1972.

New Street, 18th May 1972.

35

Kyrwicks Lane, Sparkbrook, 1972.

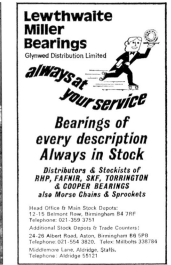

Preparations for road-widening in Hagley Road, 1972.

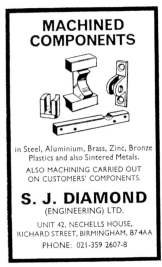

The opening of the Gravelly Hill Interchange (better known as Spaghetti Junction) by
the Rt. Hon. Peter Walker, MP, Secretary of State for the Environment, 2th May 1972.

Rear of Lansdowne Street, Winson Green, June 1972.

Tilton Road/Garrison Lane, Bordesley, 8th June 1972.

Wyndcliffe County Infants School, Little Green Lane, Small Heath, 1972.

Winson Green Road/Heath Street, 1972.

37

Birmingham Motoring Festival,
Victoria Square, 20th June 1972.

Summer Row, 1972.

Church Street, Lozells, 1972.

Victoria Square, looking towards Hill Street, 1972.

Scrapbooks, showing life in Birmingham, are ready to be sent to other United Nations countries after a presentation, by some of the children involved, to the Lord Mayor, Ald. Fred Hall, 21st July 1972.

Celebrations after Warwickshire CCC win the County Championship, 8th September 1972.

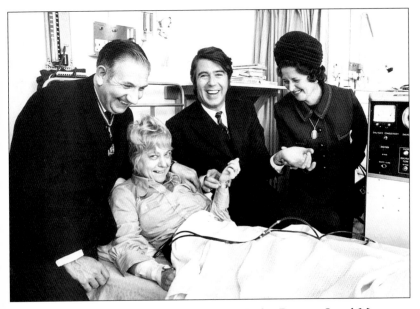

Comedian, Leslie Crowther, along with the Deputy Lord Mayor, Ald. Vic Turton, and Mrs Turton, visit Patricia Smith in the kidney unit at Queen Elizabeth Hospital, 20th September 1972.

Terry Wogan signs autographs at the opening of the Cutprice Clothing Centre, High Street, 22nd September 1972.

The Lord Mayor, Ald. Fred Hall, with members of the New Dramatic Company, prior to the Gala Reopening of the Old Repertory Theatre, Station Street, 25th September 1972. After almost sixty years as a professional theatre its main purpose, initially, was to play host to amateur companies.

Ticket collectors ready for action, Moor Street Station, 1st October 1972.

Karen Jarvis dodges the cars for the last time in Bull Street, 1st October 1972. From the following day all traffic, except buses and delivery vehicles, was to be banned as an experiment.

Lewis's staff prize-winners find an ideal way to spend their prize money, 16th November 1972. The awards were given after their examination success at Matthew Boulton Technical College.

Parkfield Road/Alum Rock Road, 1972.

BY 1973 it is estimated that the total number employed in road haulage will have risen to 240,000. This compares with 216,000 in 1968 and shows an increase of over 10 per cent.

In vehicle distribution and repair the estimated increase is even more striking, namely 30 per cent. During this five-year period 1968-1973, the number employed in this major sector of the road transport industry is expected to have risen from 345,000 to 445,000.

During the same period, however, employment in passenger transport is expected to decline 10 per cent from 263,000 to 233,000.

Picketing outside the General Hospital, Steelhouse Lane, 13th December 1972.

1973

HMS Birmingham, seen on acceptance trials on the Mersey, 1973.

Ludgate Hill. 1973.

Pershore Road, Selly Park, 4th January 1973.

Kings Road, Perry Barr, January 1973.

Wright Road, Saltley, c 1973.

Rear of The Croftway, Handsworth Wood, 1973.

Quinton Expressway, with the traffic down to a crawl, January 1973.

Court Oak Road, Harborne, 31st January 1973.

The Prime Minister, the Rt. Hon. Edward Heath, visits The University of Birmingham, February 1973.

Laundry Dept., Jaffray Hospital, Wood End Lane, Erdington, 9th March 1973.

Lichfield Road, with Grosvenor Road on the right, Aston, 1973.

Church Road, Yardley, March 1973.

Comedian, Norman Vaughan, signs autographs at the re-launch of Grey's, one of the city's oldest stores, which has just changed its name to Debenham's, Bull Street, 16th March 1973.

Thornhill Road/Stratford Road, Sparkbrook, 6th April 1973.

Coventry Road, Small Heath, April 1973.

A devastating fire at Lewis's warehouse, Aston Road, 7th April 1973.

Waterloo Road, South Yardley, May 1973.

Dignitaries at the unveiling of the new fountain.
High Street/New Street, 3rd May 1973.

Members of the Great Barr Conservative Club toast the success of Ald.
Lilian Peckover after she had won the Newtown Ward, 10th May 1973.

49

Blue Coat School, Harborne, May 1973.

Constitution Hill/Northwood Street, May 1973.

Lodge Road Congregational Church, Hockley, May 1973.

Central Library, with the new library under construction, May 1973.

Tenants from back houses in Clevedon Road meet to discuss the Council's Compulsory Purchase Order,
Balsall Heath, 20th May 1973. Almost all the houses in front of their properties had already been made derelict.

Cleo Laine

Farm Street Primary Modern School, Bridge Street West/Villa Street, Hockley, 10th July 1973.

Hagley Road West, Quinton, 1973.

Dudley Road, Spring Hill, 1973.

General Post Office, Victoria Square/Hill Street,
16th August 1973.

Temple Row, 1973.

Newhall Street, 21st August 1973.

Timberley Lane, Castle Bromwich, September 1973.

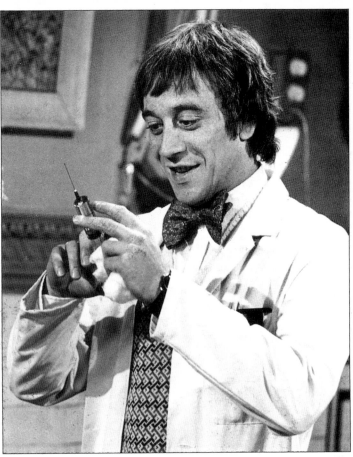
Robin Nedwell, from Stirchley, appears as Duncan Waring in the ITV sit-com, "Doctor in Charge", September 1973.

Dancers from "Carry on London", Birmingham Hippodrome, September 1973.

A burst water main causes flooding in Edward Road, Balsall Heath, 8th September 1973.

Vyse Street/Warstone Lane, Jewellery Quarter, 1973.

A tree-planting ceremony involving the Lord Mayor, Coun. Mrs Marjorie Brown, and children from Kingsland School, Kingstanding, 29th November 1973.

The Summer Hill Tavern, Summer Hill Road, 1973.

Marlene Dietrich, leaves the Alexandra Theatre after her one-woman show, 3rd December 1973.

"Robinson Crusoe" stars, Charlie Williams, Yvonne Marsh and Roy Hudd, Birmingham Hippodrome, 18th December 1973.

1974

Kingstanding Road, January 1974.

Union Street, 1974.

The Union, Berners Street, Lozells, 12th January 1974.

Great Hampton Street/Great Hampton Row, Hockley, 16th January 1974.

High Street, with Edwards Road on the right, Erdington, January 1974.

St Michael's Roman Catholic Church, New Meeting Street, January 1974.

Nelson Street Primary School, Nelson Street/King Edward's Road, 29th January 1974.

Lea Mason Church of England Secondary School, Bell Barn Road, Lee Bank, February 1974.

A recent tour of Midland Clubland by the popular comedian and TV personality **Billy Dainty** was responsible for giving valuable assistance in the treatment of cystic fibrosis at Birmingham Childrens Hospital.

During the tour, organised by Kidderminster promoter **Don Stevens** (now a top executive of show producers Leisuretime Promotions), autographed pictures of Billy Dainty were distributed to members of his audiences, each person contributing anything from 5p upwards, a total of £80 being raised in this way. This money was used by Mr. Stevens to purchase an Aerolyser. which was presented to Dr. Mary Goodchild of the Childrens Hospital.

The Lord Mayor's Annual Procession makes its way down New Street, 25th May 1974.

Billy Dainty

High Street, Harborne, 10th June 1974.

Recreation ground, rear of Granshaw Close, Kings Norton, 12th July 1974.

THE resident theatre company at Cannon Hill Arts Centre will be disbanded next month, in a financial cutback affecting all the centre's activities.

It will be replaced by a smaller company concentrating on plays for young children, and not, as at present, for adults as well.

The cutback comes at the end of the arts centre's most successful year.

Prince Albert Street/North Warwick Street, Bordesley Green, July 1974.

Witton Road, Aston, 19th July 1974.

Finalists in the "Miss Littlewood" contest line up at the Birmingham Shopping Centre, 22nd August 1974.

Northfield Road, Kings Norton, 12th September 1974.

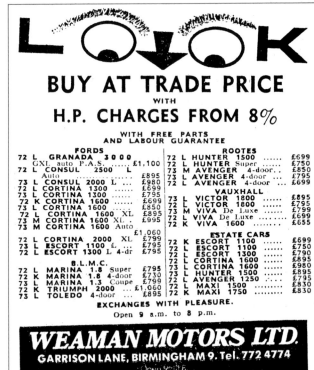
Don Maclean has created a new and entirely 'different' image to help launch his debut 'Glitarzan' on the BEEB (BBC Records) Label.

The song, written by Ray Stevens, of 'The Streak' fame, centres on a character called appropriately enough, 'Glitarzan'. He differs from Tarzan inasmuch that he swings through the trees (presumably in Don's home district of Selly Oak?) with a rather strange guitar strapped to his back!

Says Don: 'I suppose I am the jungle's answer to Garry Glitter — but far better looking!'

The record is aimed at the Christmas market and is a must for all fans of 'Crackerjack' in which Don has starred for the last two series. It's launch also heralds a particularly busy period for the comic.

On Christmas Day he will be seen as 'Wishee - Washee' in the BBC pantomime, 'Aladdin' and in January he stars in his third 'Crackerjack' series.

Bordesley Green Road/Denbigh Street, Saltley,
September 1974.

Greenhill Road/Avenue Road, Handsworth,
October 1974.

Birmingham City Speedway Team meet the Lord Mayor, Coun. Eric Eames, 22nd October 1974.

Lozells Street Primary School, Lozells Street, 1974.

Holyhead Road, Handsworth, 1974.

The pub bombings were Birmingham's greatest tragedy in the last half-century. The Mulberry Bush and Tavern in the Town were attacked by IRA bombers, New Street, 21st November 1974.

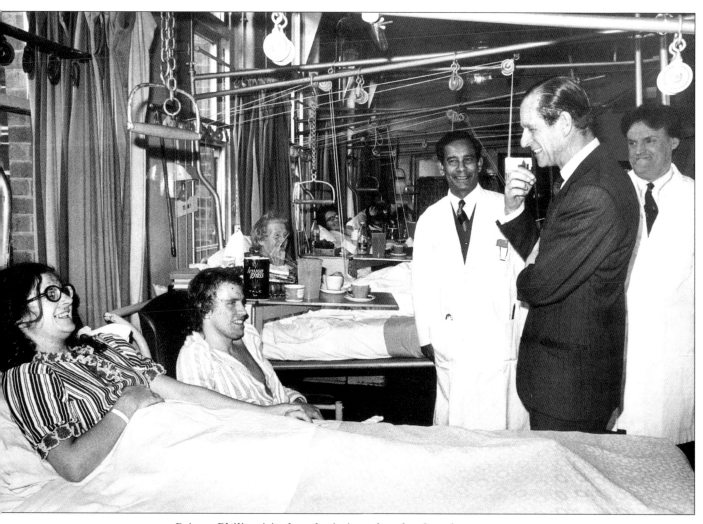

Prince Philip visits bomb victims shortly after the event.

Mike Reid

Somerset Road, Handsworth, 25th November 1974.

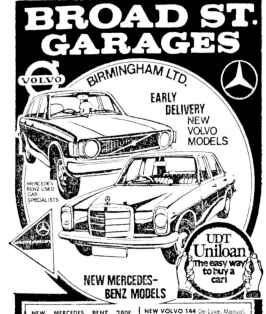

Nechells Primary School, Eliot Street, Nechells, December 1974.

A Christmas card scene in Sutton Park, c 1974.

William McGeoch and Co (B'ham) Ltd., (manufacturing electrical engineers),
Coventry Road, Small Heath, c 1975.

Model Railway Exhibition, Eddystone Radio, Alvechurch Road, West Heath, 1975.

Museum of Science and Industry, Newhall Street, c 1975.

Jamaica Row/Upper Dean Street, c 1975.

Stars of BBC TV's "It Ain't Half Hot Mum", Windsor Davies and Don Estelle, top the Hit Parade with "Whispering Grass", 1975.

Colmore Circus, Queensway, January 1975.

Charters Garage Ltd., School Lane, Yardley, January 1975.

Lionel Street, with the scene dominated by the Post Office Tower,
23rd January 1975.

70

Nursery Road, Lozells, 1975.

Booth Street, Handsworth, 1st March 1975.

Like to get your holiday off to a good start?

Easy

TAKE A 17-DAY RETURN
from
BIRMINGHAM

London	£5.81
Edinburgh/Glasgow	£11.71
Inverness	£17.02*
Llandudno	£5.72
Newquay	£9.80
Scarborough	£7.15
Torquay	£7.15
Weston-Super-Mare	£4.04

There are 17-Day Returns for most journeys over 75 miles. Go any day and return within 17 days (but if you travel out during Monday to Friday you cannot return before the following Saturday).

This ticket cannot be used on certain trains. Please check before booking.

Seat Reservations are obligatory on many Summer Friday and Saturday trains to popular resorts, and you are advised to reserve well in advance.

For full details of train services, Seat Reservations and Fare Deal bargains to these and many other destinations please ask at principal British Rail stations or Appointed Travel Agents or ring BIRMINGHAM 643 2711.

Inter-City makes the going easy

Warwick Road, Tyseley, 18th March 1975.

Albert Road, Stechford, 13th June 1975.

BIRMINGHAM teachers are leading a move for minimum salaries of £50 a week.

They want a teachers' salary of not less than £2,500 a year to be a priority in the next salaries claim for the profession.

Members of the National Union of Teachers' Birmingham association will call for the move at the union's Easter conference at Blackpool.

CONGRATULATIONS to the Castle Bromwich lorry-drivers who gave the money they collected for the Birmingham bomb victims direct to them.

The moral of this is to ignore all official pleas for disaster funds and collect in groups, roads and so on.

Select two or three in that group and deliver personally to the people who need the money.

No official committee — just a group of their own.

The result Happiness in the knowledge that the money given so generously is going at once where it was intended.

Botch-up

Bournville.

Acocks Green Island, 1975.

Boldmere Road, Sutton Coldfield, 1975.

Keeper's Pool, Sutton Park, c 1975.

The Queen arrives to open the Mason College
Centenary Exhibition, The University of Birmingham,
27th June 1975.

Alcester Road, Moseley, 15th July 1975.

BIRMINGHAM SHOW

THE SHOW OF THE YEAR
PERRY PARK

Situated alongside M.6 Motorway (Exit No. 7)
29th and 30th AUGUST 1975

MAGNIFICENT
FLOWER SHOW

INCLUDING DISPLAYS BY LEADING EXHIBITORS
(Flower Show Marquees open 10.30 a.m.—10.00 p.m. Friday;
9.00 a.m.—7.00 p.m. Saturday)

CHAMPIONSHIP RABBIT SHOW
BEES AND HONEY SHOW
HORSE SHOW
CAGE BIRD SHOW
AGRICULTURAL EXHIBIT
CHAMPIONSHIP DOG SHOW

SPINNING AND WEAVING DEMONSTRATIONS
AQUARIA EXHIBIT—TRADE SUNDRIES
PARADE OF SHIRES

ARENA ATTRACTIONS—Including

R.A.F. Police Dogs
West Midlands Police Musical Ride (Sat.)

ADMISSION (including V.A.T.)

	FRIDAY		SATURDAY	
		In Advance		In Advance
10.0 a.m.	70p	50p	9.0 a.m.	50p	40p
3.0 p.m.	50p	35p	2.0 p.m.	45p	35p
7.0 p.m.	25p	—	7.0 p.m.	15p	—

Children (under 15 years) 15p all day Friday and up to 7.0 p.m.
Saturday; 10p from 7.0 p.m.

ALL DAY FRIDAY AT THE GATE ONLY 20p Old Age Pensioners
**Party Bookings Two Free Tickets with each block of 25 purchased
in Advance**

Reception Class, St Vincent's R.C. Primary School, Nechells, 1975.

Waterloo Road/Stechford Road, South Yardley, 1975.

The collapse of a café, fortunately with no casualties, brings the Fire Brigade into action, Vittoria Street/Warstone Lane, Jewellery Quarter, 25th September 1975.

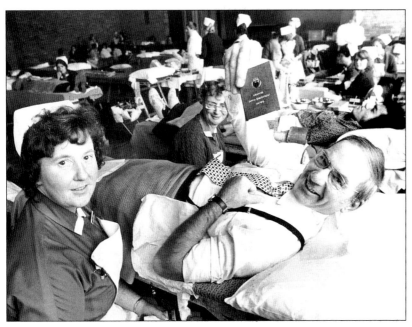

Coun. Albert Jackson becomes the first Lord Mayor to give blood when he assists the students' annual donor session at Aston University, 30th October 1975.

Members of the Sparkbrook Tenants Action Group stage a protest in a campaign to get rid of a derelict building at the junction of Farm Road and Stratford Road, 14th November 1975.

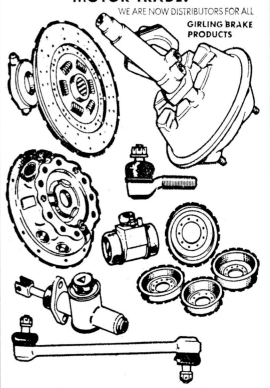

Birmingham FC recently had comedian Bill Wayne (of Dailey & Wayne) join them in a training session at Elmdon in a bid to shed some weight from his 15 stone frame! It resulted in Bill having to be carried from the field by goalkeeper Dave Latchford and striker Kenny Burns. Bill, who once took a trial for Manchester United is now devoted to show business. At the weekend he and his partner Pat Dailey go to New Zeland Australia and the USA on a tour.

Ronald Place/Cherrywood Road, Bordesley Green, 20th November 1975.

Kingstanding Road, Kingstanding, December 1975.

Colmore Row/Temple Row West, c 1975.

A bird's eye-view of the Bull Ring, 1975.

1976

The Golden Eagle, Hill Street, 1976.

Preparations underway for the building of the railway station at The University of Birmingham, 1976.

Lionel Street, with the Shakespeare Public House on the right, 1976.

Villa Road/Hamstead Road, Handsworth, 1976.

Cannon Street, c 1976.

Oxhill Road, Handsworth, 5th January 1976.

Kingsbury Road, Erdington, 1976.

Alltyres Service Ltd., Bradford Street/Mill Lane, Deritend, January 1976.

Bridge demolition in Lifford Lane, Kings Norton, c 1976.

Oak Tree Lane, Selly Oak, 6th January 1976.

SUPERTONIC!
Concorde takes off...and dreams become reality

A MESSAGE FROM MRS MARGARET THATCHER, M P

The National Exhibition Centre is an outstanding example of what can be achieved by co-operation.

It will be a lasting symbol of British enterprise. As exhibitions and conferences become increasingly international in character; it is right that we should have the best possible facilities in this country.

Britain was for many years "the workshop of the world." This splendid new development will provide a shop window for the world.

The Queen and Duke of Edinburgh at the opening of the National Exhibition Centre, 2nd February 1976.

The cheese counter, Rackhams, 1976.

Birmingham-born skating champion, John Curry, proudly holds his Olympic medal aloft at the
Boat and Leisure Life Exhibition, Bingley Hall, 18th February 1976.

Bristol Street Motors, Coventry Road, Hay Mills, March 1976.

Ideal Garage Service Station (B'ham) Ltd., Bromford Lane, Ward End, 1976.

Winson Street, Winson Green, 1976.

Gravelly Hill North, with Cecil Road on the right, Erdington, c 1976.

Havelock Road, Saltley, 29th April 1976.

City of Birmingham Education Committee Depot (repair branch), Kyotts Lake Road, Sparkbrook, July 1976.

Princess Anne pauses to speak to the cleaning staff, after officially opening the Wholesale Markets Precinct,
13th October 1976.

King Alfred Place (now part of the ICC site) 1976.

Formans Road, Sparkhill, 1976.

The Matchmaker, The Meadway, Garretts Green, 1976.

The Gaumont Cinema, Colmore Circus, (showing "The Omen", starring Gregory Peck), 12th November 1976.

High Street, Erdington, c 1976.

Jayne and Ann Jobson and Debbie Green raise funds for the Sunday Mercury's "Give A Girl Health" Fund with their own version of "Rumpelstiltskin", Sutton Coldfield, 19th December 1976.

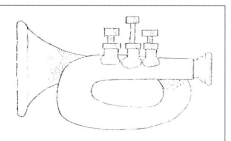

Children from local authority homes are welcomed to the Hippodrome by the Lord Mayor, Coun. Harold Powell, 31st December 1976. It was part of the annual treat laid on by members of the Birmingham Licensed Taxi Owners and Drivers Association.

Anticipating the Queen's celebrations, in June, one of the three official Silver Jubilee buses receives a send-off on its tour of the city, 8th January 1977.

Protesters demonstrate to demand a 30 mph speed limit for vehicles, Pinfold Lane, Great Barr, 2nd February 1977.

Millward Street/Green Lane, Small Heath, 1977.

The Green, Kings Norton, c 1977.

Asian refugees, thanks to links with Ugandan businesses, are entertained by Chipperfield's Circus,
Bingley Hall, 5th February 1977.

The residents of Thaxstead Road have organised a trip to Weston-Super-Mare for children from the Tile Cross area, White Hart public house, 22nd May 1977.

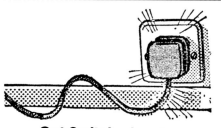

Shaftmoor Lane, Hall Green, 1977.

Springfield Road, Moseley, May 1977.

St Paul's, Moseley Road, Balsall Heath, 23rd May 1977.

93

Queen's Silver Jubilee Thanksgiving Celebrations,
Meriden Way, Kingshurst, 7th June 1977.

Flooding in Pershore Road, Stirchley, 14th June 1977.

Sutton Coldfield's Jim Peverelle rehearses for a
spectacular event at the NEC, 19th June 1977.

Canal Boat Rally, looking towards Oozells Street, c 1977.

Knightlow Road, Harborne, 1977.

Steam fans turn out to say goodbye to Pendennis Castle after her trip from Birmingham to Didcot, 14th July 1977. The train had been sold to an Australian company.

A contrasting view, a glimpse of two different worlds, just off Icknield Street, Ladywood, July 1977.

The Royal Marine Commando Military Band entertain the crowds as they await the Queen's arrival, Victoria Square, 27th July 1977.

The Queen, in Victoria Square, as part of her Silver Jubilee celebrations, 27th July 1977.

Members of Hawkesley Estate Community Club committee meet the Lord Mayor, Coun. Freda Cocks, her consort, Mr Cocks, and the chairman of the Housing Committee, Coun. Arthur Walker, during their visit to Kings Norton, 7th September 1977.

During the bread shortage Richard's Bakers somehow manages to conjure up 1200 loaves, between 9am and 11am, St Stephens Road/Pershore Road, Stirchley, 10th September 1977.

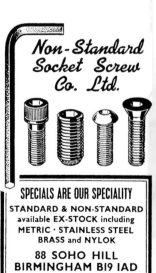
Market porters give their support to the Jubilee Harvest Festival with a gift of fruit to be distributed to deserving causes, St Martin's, 27th September 1977.

Birmingham Shopping Centre (now The Pallasades) from Corporation Street, October 1977.

Father Christmas arrives at Lewis's, 5th November 1977.

Striking firemen march to the Town Hall to vote on a peace formula, New Street, 13th December 1977.

Elton John appears in concert
on BBC TV, 7th November 1977.

Comedian, Terry Scott, is welcomed, as part of the
Birmingham Mail Christmas Tree Fund events,
organised by BRMB Radio, 17th December 1977.

Beckbury Road, Weoley Castle, 1978.

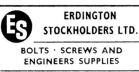

101

Woolworth's assistants celebrate their annual pay rise, which ensures that anyone aged over 20 will earn at least £2000 a year, Bull Ring, 5th January 1978.

Danny La Rue, with his team of singers, dancers, musicians and backstage staff, prepares for a week of performances at the Night Out, Horse Fair, 12th January 1978.

Members of the Birmingham branch of the Elvis Presley Fan Club about to take part in the "Miss Elvis Presley" Competition at the Golden Eagle in Hill Street, 12th February 1978.

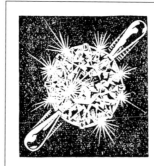

Coventry Road, with George Road on the right, Hay Mills, 9th March 1978.

The Royal Navy Display Team performs as part of the 1000th BBC TV
"Pebble Mill at One" programme, 20th March 1978.

Grove Lane, between Osborne Road and Leyton Road, Handsworth,
April 1978.

Tyseley Railway Museum, 1978.

Wesleyan and General Assurance Society Honours Club Members, Midland Hotel, 13th April 1978.

Staff at St Vincent's R.C. Primary School, Nechells, 1978.

Harborne Hill cricket team, 1978.

Part of the Welsh House Farm School Spring Festival, Quinton, 25th May 1978.

BUCKINGHAM PALACE

13th June, 1978

Dear Mrs Johnson,

The Queen has asked me to thank you for your charming and most informative letter of 24th May.

Her Majesty is delighted that the Pheasey Over-Sixty Club is thriving, and that your two hundred members decided to have a Thanksgiving Service on the 11th June. The Queen particularly wishes me to say that she hopes that all your celebrations have met with the greatest possible success and warmly reciprocates your good wishes.

Yours sincerely

Robert Fellowes

Mrs. H. Johnson.

Don't be fooled – this glamorous party is made up entirely of members of the Asman Boys' Club, Moseley, 15th June 1978. They were taking part in the annual village festival.

Moseley Village Green, 1978.

Westminster Road/Hutton Road, Handsworth, 1978.

SCHOOLBOY Simon Rudd is Britain's youngest business tycoon . . . at only 10.

He is a shareholder in a Midland firm with a £1,000,000-a-year turnover and has just got shares in a new company.

Within two years. Simon is expected to be earning about £5,000 a year from his shares. The cash will go in his own bank account.

As an active shareholder, Simon, of Four Oaks. Sutton Coldfield, turns up at the firm on Saturday mornings to help with the loading and writing out price cards.

Simon got a stake in the Coventry-based fancy goods wholesalers Carter and Rowland when his father, Mr. Christopher Rudd, bought it for £100,000 last year.

Now Simon has got shares with his father's second firm, a cash and carry warehouse, Centasave, in Stratford Road, Sparkhill, Birmingham.

For Simon it is a child's dream . . . the warehouse is stacked high with cut-price toys.

Mr. Rudd, aged 47, got a half share in £1,000,000 when he and his brother John sold their D I Y chain of Calypso stores in the Midlands three years ago.

Other shareholders in the two companies include Mr. Rudd's wife, Ann; 16-year-old daughter Joanne and 14-year-old Christopher.

Mr. Rudd was only 10 when he first started helping his own father in his D I Y shop in Smethwick.

SMASH-HIT shows like "My Fair Lady," "South Pacific" and the "Sound of Music," are to come the way of Birmingham theatres.

"My Fair Lady" will lead the way when it opens at Birmingham Hippodrome for three weeks next April.

Sumptuous revivals of the big musicals were announced in London today by the Arts Council and Moss Empires as a move to help to keep regional theatres alive.

The production of "My Fair Lady," expected to star Birmingham-born Tony Britton as Professor Higgins, will open in Leicester on November 9.

It will then play in provincial theatres for six months — at a cost of more than £500,000.

"I hope the venture will give a new lease of life to the theatres," said Mr. Louis Benjamin, managing director of Moss Empires.

Barbara Hanna, Queen of the Bournville Festival, with her courtiers, 24th June 1978.

Gravelly Industrial Park, 1978.

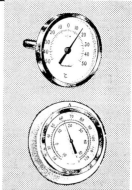

You can almost feel the cold in the Bull Ring market, 21st December 1978.

1979

The opening of W. Canning & Co. Ltd. (makers of electro-platers' and polishers' plant and materials and lacquer manufacturers) extension, Great Hampton Street, c 1979.

High Street, Harborne, 1979.

Alcester Road South, Kings Heath, 1979.

The new vicar of Mere Green, the Rev Keith Punshon, sets out with his flock from St James's Church, 29th January 1979.

Garrison Lane, Bordesley Green, February 1979.

Rookery Road, Handsworth, 1979.

Dunlop white-collar workers stage a mass walk-out in protest over job cutbacks, Fort Dunlop, 5th February 1979.

W. Canning & Co. Ltd. football team, 1978/79.

Comedians, Lenny Henry and Don Maclean, aided by bearded driver John Hudgell, launch the world's biggest ambulance, Grand Hotel, Colmore Row, 30th March 1979. The vehicle was then used to transport handicapped people on pilgrimages, holidays and tours across Europe.

Birmingham Councillors, led by the Lord Mayor, Coun. Edward Hanson, at full stretch as they limber up as part of the City Slickers football team, Victoria Square, 16th April 1979.

All Soul's Parish Church, Wenlock Road/Norris Road, Aston, 1979.

Gene Relph uses an old barrel to negotiate the
flooded Witton Road, Witton, 31st May 1979.

First Holy Communion at St Dunstan's RC Primary School, Drayton Road, Kings Heath, 1979.

Holy Trinity Church, Trinity Road, Birchfield, June 1979.

Airport expansion plans spark off a protest, 1st August 1979.

Bath Row, 1979.

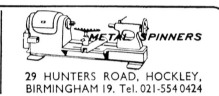

Stephenson Place, September 1979.

High Street, Deritend, 1979.

Travelling display from Tyseley Railway Museum, supervised by Keith Shakespeare (right),
Bromyard, 1979.

Rear of Bath Row Garage, Lee Bank, c 1979.

Bull Ring, 15th September 1979.

Father Christmas makes a triumphant arrival ten weeks early! Debenhams, Bull Street,
26th October 1979.

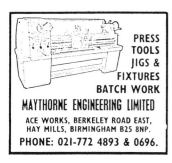

Next month sees the end of a thirteen year residency for the Bobby Johnson
Band at the Tower Ballroom, Edgbaston, December 1979.

Chefs from the Metropole Hotel watch as the Lord Mayor, Coun. George Canning, cuts the first slice,
at the ox-roast, to raise funds for the East Birmingham Hospital Leukaemia Ward Fund,
Bull Ring Shopping Centre, 20th December 1979.

Back Cover: The statue of King Kong dominates the scene in Manzoni Gardens, Bull Ring, 14th May 1972. It was loaned to the city, for six months, by the Peter Stuyvesant Foundation but, although it was offered as a permanent fixture, the council refused to purchase it. For a while it inhabited a used car site in Camp Hill.

ACKNOWLEDGEMENTS

(for providing photographs, for encouragement and numerous other favours)

Norman Bailey; Jim Banks; The Birmingham City Council Dept. of Planning and Architecture; The Birmingham Post and Mail Ltd.; Ron Butler; Dave and Kath Carpenter; Dave Coles; Joan Dainty; Balraj Dhingsa; Alan Foster; Joyce Gill; International Print Shop; Anne Jennings; Barbara Kemp; Tony Kent; Joyce Lockwood; Dennis Moore; George Peace; Keith Pipkin; Arnold Price; Douglas Price; Mike Reid, Keith Shakespeare; Joan Wanty; Joan Ward; Joan Wilkes; Rosemary Wilkes; Eric Williamson; Ken Windsor.

Please forgive any possible omissions. Every effort has been made to include all organisations and individuals involved in the book.

A snarl-up, involving prams, at the opening of Woolworth's, Chelmsley Wood, 26th February 1971.